ask the circle
to forgive you

Nichita Stănescu

ask the circle to forgive you

Selected Poems
1964-1979

Translated from the Romanian
by Mark Irwin & Mariana Carpinisan

The Globe Press

1983

Cleveland · New York · London

First published in Romania

Starea Poeziei, Editura Minerva, © 1975
Epica Magna, Editura Junimea, © 1978
Operele Imperfecte, Editura Albatros, © 1979

Translations © 1982 Mark Irwin and Mariana Carpinisan
Introduction © 1982 Mark Irwin

First Published in English in 1983 by

The Globe Press

18803 North Park Blvd.
Cleveland, Ohio 44122

736 West End Ave. 2-C
New York, N.Y. 10025

Titles also available from:

Small Press Distribution
1784 Shattuck Ave.
Berkeley, CA 94709

Library of Congress Catalogue Number: 82-84247
ISBN: 0-910321-05-1 (paper)
ISBN: 0-910321-06-X
Cover design by Mihai Iordache

First Edition

Acknowledgements

Special thanks to the editors of the following periodicals in which many of these
translations originally appeared:

Ardis Anthology of East European Poetry (University of Michigan Press), *The
Iowa Review, Ironwood, Modern Poetry in Translation* (London), *New Directions,
Pequod, Seneca Review, World Literature Today.*

I would like to thank the Fulbright Committee for a Fellowship to Romania during
which time some of these translations were completed.

M.I.

Contents

Introduction   7
Preface   13

I.   The State of Poetry
     Embrace   16
     Sentimental Story   17
     Poem   18
     Song   19
     Adolescents on the Sea   20
     Sad Love Song   21
     Marina   22
     Winter Ritual   23
     Ferns   24
     A Wall   25
     Endscape   26
     To Hypnos   27
     Poetry   31
     Last Supper   32
     Poem   33
     Oh, If . . .   34
     On the Top Floor   35
     Injustice   36

II. The Eleven Elegies
     The Eleventh Elegy   40

III. Epica Magna
     Her   48
     Confession   50
     Why?   51
     Contemplating the World from the Outside   52
     The Sky's Mistake   61
     Hieroglyphics   62

IV. Imperfect Works
     Lesson on the Cube   66
     Talking   67
     Untitled   68
     The Keys   69
     Transfiguration of the Face   70
     Engagement   71
     The Ghost   72
     The Lark   73
     Lesson on the Circle   74

INTRODUCTION

The work of Nichita Stănescu is a poetry of immaculate rituals, illuminations which range from the colorful landscapes of his native Romanian folklore to the ravaged endscapes of postwar Europe. There are weddings, transfigurations, last suppers, and lessons in which objects are metamorphosed into the human, embarrassing us with our own vulnerability.

lesson on the circle

On the sand you draw a circle
which you divide in two,
with the same stick of almond you divide that in two.
Then you fall on your knees,
and then you fall on your arms.
And after that you strike your forehead on the sand
and ask the circle to forgive you.
So much.

These poems are epistemologies, interrogations whose concern is to name things, to unveil their origin and nature, wherein we glimpse what is stubbornly mortal.

talking

Do you think the grass is happy?
It is green; it is green . . .
Do you think the eagle is high?
He is flying; he is flying . . .
Do you think the stone is silent?
It is hard; it is hard . . .
Do you think that I am yours?
Do you think so?

One marvels at the ease with which the poet approaches the metaphysical, whether the vehicle be humor or pain.

From the stars a chain of keys fell through my brain,
my mind was a jingle of pain and sound.
My entire body became a key of iron,

(the keys)

The immediacy of these poems is startling. First lines are textured with a visual and auditory magic (stars . . . chain of keys) that captures the intolerable yet mortal condition of accepting that which is infinite and beyond. People are transformed into things, man is viewed and consumed by nature,

Ferns, oh you ferns!
Come and drink me with such a dry snout
that you cannot scream any longer.

(Ferns)

or nature is depicted as *imperfect* so that one might more easily approach, becoming wonderfully confused in its whole.

All over the sky
vultures were flying upside down
and their spines fell
touching my chest.

My flesh was their sky,
the light from my eyes
their earth.

(the sky's mistake)

It is impossible to consider Stănescu's poetry without discussing his sophisticated perspective of time, for in this aspect he enters the forefront of European poetry. One can most easily grasp this perspective through the poem "Song," and in Part II of "Contemplating the World from the Outside." In the former poem, the temporal scheme is moved forward: the past is hopelessly beyond us and should only be examined in the present's context.

Only this moment has memories.
What happened before no one knows.

8

Since death is a communion with the present in that it freezes the moment, the dead take part in that eternal present.

> The dead still exchange among them
> names, numbers, one, two, three . . .

Yet for mortals the present seems elusive; it escapes us, who can only approach it occasionally, in such terms as Eliot presents in "The Dry Salvages."

> For most of us, there is only the unattended
> Moment, the moment in and out of time,
> The distraction fit, lost in a shaft of sunlight . . .

The future, however, also shares this communion with the present in that its gradual focus lies there.

> Only what will be exists,
> only the unhappened happenings,
> hanging from the branch of a tree
> unborn, half ghost . . .

The speaker's "sadness," an emotion we most often associate with the past, is wonderfully confused with what has not yet happened and thus distills the poem's final dictum: only those who dwell in the present are capable of effecting the future.

> My sadness listens to the unborn dogs
> barking at unborn men.
> Only they are going to exist!
> We, inhabitants of this second,
> we are a dream of the night, slender,
> with thousands of legs running everywhere.

Yet it is in "Contemplating the World from the Outside," in which the earth is viewed as a distant sphere, that Stănescu consummates his theory of time preserved through song, because it is song that enters the *degree zero* of being, the present where all events are made possible because they commune with that nothingness from which everything is molded.

This is the only tragic place
because the number one rules,
and not zero,

Part II (The Divine Nerve)

It is through song (the Orphic notion of dismemberment, fragmentation in order to become part of the whole *zero cycle* of nature) that the ceaseless notion of time becomes undone and thus advances the theme of regeneration, "The still unborn about the dead," from the earlier *Eleven Elegies*.

3. *The Song*

It interrupts
any other move.

It makes that which exists
vanish
makes appear in being
what is still unborn.

It is through the individual act of singing that the temporally infinite and spatially human intersect through the spirit, enabling the poet to construct a universe with the word.

It swings death
until words bloom
and adorn the laws of fixed stars
with tears.
This at times is called the soul,
but it would be even more precise to call it
song.

For the Western reader, the oddity of these poems will appear not so much in their abstractions as in their absurd nature, a notion long prevalent in Romanian art, yet most publicly known through the work of Eugen Ionescu in theater, and Constantin Brancuşi in sculpture. The reader should note that certain images, which might appear sentimental or overly romantic to our eyes, are often meant to be both humorous and mockingly serious. Yet despite cultural differences, we are most often seduced, marveling at the truth and sheer honesty of these poems.

Spune-mi, dacă te-aş prinde-ntr-o zi
şi ţi-aş săruta talpa piciorului,
nu-i aşa că ai şchiopăta puţin, după aceea,
de teamă să nu-mi striveşti sărutul ?...

Tell me, if one day I catch you
and kiss the sole of your foot,
afterwards, won't you limp a little
in fear of crushing that kiss? . . .

Mark Irwin
Bucharest 1981

PREFACE

The translations which appear in this text are arranged, for the most part, in the chronological order in which they were originally published. It should be noted that the first section of this book contains poems from *Starea Poeziei,* a *Selected Poems* itself, which draws from 13 books published between 1960 and 1972. The *Eleven Elegies* were published as a complete book in 1966. My decision to include "The Eleventh Elegy" is based on the consideration that, of all the elegies, this is a complete poem in itself. Like "Contemplating the World from the Outside," it presents a miniature universe complete with geography, inhabitants, and philosophy. In this manner, Stănescu's architecture might be compared with that of Gabriel García Márquez, most notably in his work *One Hundred Years of Solitude.* Aurel Martin, a prominent Romanian critic, has suggested this original hierarchy of things might only be termed *nichitastănescian.*

My familiarity with the Romanian language is rudimentary: a basic grasp of vocabulary, syntax, and structure, most of which was acquired while working with Ms. Carpinisan during the three-year span of this project. She is a native Romanian with a thorough knowledge of English. Without her, the work would not have been possible. I would also like to thank Damian Necula and the author himself for their help in Bucharest. There, our common language was French.

Occasionally, Mr. Stănescu prefers to omit end-line punctuation, usually the comma or period. At times, however, in poems where the end-line punctuation seems to have been omitted altogether, the author uses the comma in a particular line for emphasis, or to denote apposition. The best example of this occurs in the poem "Poetry." There are similar occasions in the long poems. I have tried to adhere to these standards which, although not grammatically consistent, seem to function through a more intuitive logic. The Romanian texts, however, are consistent; similarly punctuated poems usually appear in the same volume.

Finally, I have only presented those poems which work as *poems* in English. The literal meaning and structure of every poem has been preserved. Those poems which sounded like translations, without the complete re-casting of certain metaphors, I have preferred to leave out.

M.I.

ONE

a selection from

Starea Poeziei

The State of Poetry
Selected Poems
1960-1972

EMBRACE

When we catch sight of each other,
the air casts between us
a sudden image of trees,
moving, indifferent and naked.

Calling each other's name,
we are thrown together so fast,
that between our breasts, time collapses,
and the hour struck, breaks into minutes.

I would have liked to hold you
like the held body of childhood,
with each of its unrepeated deaths.
And with my ribs would have embraced you.

SENTIMENTAL STORY

Meeting more and more often,
I sat on one edge of the hour,
you—on the other,
like two handles of an amphora.
Only the words flying between us
back and forth,
their turnings almost seen;
then, falling on one knee,
I stuck my elbow into the earth
to see the grass
bent at the downfall of a word,
as if under the paw of a running lion.
Words were circling among us, back and forth,
back and forth,
and the more I loved you, the more
as a twist almost seen,
the words were rehearsing
the structure of the universe,
from the beginning.

POEM

Tell me, if one day I catch you
and kiss the sole of your foot,
afterwards, won't you limp a little
in fear of crushing that kiss? . . .

SONG

Only this moment has memories.
What happened before no one knows.
The dead still exchange among them
names, numbers, one, two, three . . .
Only what will be exists,
only the unhappened happenings,
hanging from the branch of a tree ˙
unborn, half ghost . . .
Only my stiffened body exists,
the last of the old, of stone.
My sadness listens to the unborn dogs
barking at unborn men.
Only they are going to exist!
We, inhabitants of this second,
we are a dream of the night, slender,
with thousands of legs running everywhere.

ADOLESCENTS ON THE SEA

The sea is covered with adolescents
who, standing, learn how to walk on waves,
resting their arms on the currents,
making use of the sun's stiff rays.
I lie, watching from the shore's
perfect angle which they seemingly approach.
An infinite fleet. And I wait
to see a wrong step, at least
a slip up to the knee, into the gauze of breaking waves
that sound under their slow advance.
But they are slender and calm, having now
learned how to walk on the waves, standing.

SAD LOVE SONG

Yes, only my life will die for me
sometime.
Only the grass knows the earth's taste.
Yes, only my blood is sad
when it goes away from the heart.
The air is tall, you are tall,
my sadness is tall.
A time is coming when horses die.
A time is coming when machinery grows old.
A time is coming when it rains coldly
and all the women wear your face,
and your dresses.
And a great white bird is coming
and lays the moon on the sky.

MARINA

Nothing is left. Nothing can be recognized,
presumed or supposed.
Behind me, a horse made of nothing, still grazing
on the nameless and invisible grass.
Ahead, the view becomes clearer,
the glance suspended with fishing lines
occasionally jerked by a fish made of light
which you eat, then throw the skeleton away:
or plant in the place of a fir tree on a mountain
submerged in the sea; where you fall through
the weight of a long and purple cloud
made of drowned bodies.

WINTER RITUAL

Always a cupola,
another one always.
Taking on a halo like a saint,
or only a rainbow.
Your straight body, my straight body
as during a wedding.
A wise priest made of air
is facing us with two wedding bands.
You lift your left hand, I lift my left arm:
our smiles mirror each other.
Your friends and my friends are crying
syllabic tears like Christmas carols.
They take pictures as we kiss.
Lightning. Darkness. Lightning. Darkness.
I lower one knee and fall on my arms.
I kiss your ankle with sadness.
I take your shoulder, you take my waist,
and majestically we enter the winter.
Your friends and my friends step aside.
A ton of snow overturns on us.
We die freezing. And once again, only the locks of hair
adorn our skeletons in spring.

FERNS

Green cells which flow under stones.
Ferns, oh you ferns!
Come and drink me with such a dry snout
that you cannot scream any longer.

Ferns, oh you ferns! Green milk
consumed by the mouth of winter.
Come and drink me with frozen snout,
icebergs overturn beneath the sky.

Now they are by the star
called Canopus, and the moon.
Ferns, oh you ferns!
Bones of the cold, foam.

A WALL

Curved wall, full of hooks,
where eagles with soft necks hang.
Oblique wall, full of hooks
stuck in the eyes of dead children.
Triangular wall, full of hooks,
where swords with red blades hang.
Square wall, full of hooks,
where bows that are rusted hang.
Broken wall, full of hooks,
where my veins like ropes hang.
Curved wall, oblique wall,
triangular and square wall, full of hooks,
on which always, something is hanging . . .

ENDSCAPE

Mud which smears, gracious mud,
mud left by words in the air,
mud dressing the first step detached
from earth, on a bridge made of air.

Mud up to the windows, up to the locks,
mud shaped like keys having seeped into rooms,
keys opening the huge door of silence,
found in each vacant hour.

Mud of meaningless seconds,
of hostile silence surrounding
the old dead who died happy.

Flowing mud, made of gracious animals
harnessed to a plow of bone, livid,
plowing our flesh within,
sows it with hungry skulls
of those dead before our birth,
continually growing.

TO HYPNOS

I.

They were asleep. They were born asleep;
words were screaming in their sleep,
they were born from their last syllables.

They grew sleeping, fell in love
sleeping and celebrated
their wedding while asleep.

In their sleep, they established places for words.
Their women gave birth sleeping,
and all of them grew old
while asleep
and died this way.

The youth, sleeping, took their place
in dream,
we and the heart-rending words asleep
replaced the old, profound words
that were asleep.

II.

But for them to wake up,
this,
no one wants.

They were alive in sleep because
only in dream
were they living within their body.

Their birds were flying asleep,
their fish swimming asleep,
their horses galloping asleep,
and in vineyards during autumn,
grapes of dream were ripening.

Nobody, no one wants to wake up,
because only in this way
is their form their own,
entirely, and all at once.

III.

They hated the ones awake.
They said that the ones awake
don't live in themselves.

They said that the ones awake
are only what is seen when they see,
only what is heard, when they hear,
only the pain felt when they feel pain.

They hated the ones awake.
They said that the ones awake
are not able to live
inside their bodies
but,
because they, the ones awake, would be empty
inside,
they are always running
within themselves
being, time after time
only an ankle
or only a temple
or only an arm,—
the rest of their body thrown back
time after time in the dark.

IV.

They hate the ones awake
calling them
"The ones without body."

But sometimes
their hate became colossal
because they said,
that even sight can wake up
and then the colors don't live any longer,
even hearing can wake up
and then the sounds don't live any longer

And even the colors can wake up
and then
their vibrations
don't live any longer

Even the sound can wake up
and then
the memories
don't live any longer . . .

Even the pain can wake up
and then
the memories
don't live any longer . . .

V.

They were asleep. They were born asleep.
They were multiplying asleep.
Dying asleep.
But all this time
identical with their body.

They were alive in dream
and even the trees
in order to shade them
had to fall asleep,
being able, only in this way,
to cast over their entire bodies
the shadow of their roots.

POETRY

Poetry is the eye that cries
It is the shoulder that cries
the eye of the shoulder that cries
It is the hand that cries
the eye of the hand that cries
It is the foot that cries
the eye of the heel that cries
Oh you, friends,
poetry is not a tear
but the crying itself
crying of an undiscovered eye
the tear of an eye
of one supposed to be beautiful,
the tear of one supposed to be happy.

LAST SUPPER

House with moving walls
with rooms traveling into each other
Beneath the feathers of a bird
the ceilings cross the sea to Malta
Room with a long table
with chairs, scales of a coiled snake
I sit at the end, at the wedding,
with one foot I step out of my myth
Oh, and above, what a torrential rain with heads,
beheaded heads, snub-nosed ones, old ones,
rain of the night, on the empty floor
roaring rain, lasting weeks
Give me your hand, my frightened bride,
and let's run, let's run together
Soon it will rain with bodies
and the vault will fall on us.
It will rain with beheaded heads
Let's run, let's run you and me,
from the house with walls forever moving
where our last supper took place . . .

POEM

Yet still, this remains the most important,—
the old tree which others have seen,
the first woman, which others have loved,
the first stone, which others have turned into stone . . .
Yet still, that you can never return,
because others returned you
remains the most important,
always others and others, and others,
until that *you* does not recognize *you*,—
they cross paths, they mix with others . . .

OH, IF . . .

Oh, if I could say that I have another soul,
after I lost my body,
                            to say
that I have another soul for the horse, for instance,
for the horse you trained.

Ah, if I could have just a little,
                            —of the flower's scent—
under my dirty armpit
with which I cover the dead, saying:
Don't talk, it's not time yet,
don't talk, it is not time!—
. . . but all this while the time passes
and the only soul I have
eats time, never having enough . . .

ON THE TOP FLOOR

Now, she lives alone on the top floor;
her delicate smell flickers,
the town departs—harnessed to hungry
and vagabond dogs

Let's lay out some bread for the sparrows
and our dry and crumbled bodies
let's lay them out
for the starving silver beaks
of the unspoken gods

More pity for the rising stars,
more compassion for the ray
of moonlight,
more cold for the frozen stones
and me,
me, for me—more air.
I smother; more air!

INJUSTICE

Why should we hear and why should we have ears
to listen?
Are we so sinful that
we have
to have
hopes for beauty
eyes for tenderness
and legs for running?
Are we indeed so unhappy
that we have to love each other?
Are we so unstable
that we have to prolong
through birth
our ugly sadness
and our eager love?

TWO

a selection from

"11 ELEGII"

The Eleven Elegies
1966

THE ELEVENTH ELEGY
Entry into spring labors

I.

Heart greater than the body, leaping
from all sides at once
and collapsing from all sides
back onto the body
like a storm of lava,

heart, content greater than form, this is
knowledge of self, this is
why matter is born from itself, struggling,
so that it is able to die.
Only he who knows himself dies.
Only he who is his own witness
is born.

I should run, I told myself,
but first I should
turn my soul
towards my motionless ancestors,
withdrawn into the towers of their bones,
like marrow, motionless
as things brought to an end.

I can run because they are in me.
I will run, because only what
is motionless within
can move,
only he who is alone within
has company; and knows that his heart, unseen,
will more strongly collapse
towards its own
center

                    or,
broken up into planets, allow itself to be touched
by animals and plants,
                              or,
stretched out, lie under pyramids
as if behind a foreign chest.

II.

Everything is simple, so simple that
it becomes incomprehensible.

Everything is close, so
close that
it draws back behind the eyes
and cannot be seen.

Everything is so perfect
in the spring
that only by surrounding it with myself
am I aware of it,
as I am aware of the sprouting of grass, a knowledge
confessed by words to the mouth,
confessed by the mouth to the heart,
by the heart to its core
which within itself is motionless,
like the earth's core
stretching all around itself
an infinity of gravitation's arms,

embracing everything at once
in such a strong embrace
that movement escapes through its arms.

III.

I will run, then, in all directions
at once, after my own heart
I will run like a chariot
pulled from all sides at once
by a herd of whipped horses.

IV.

I will run till the movement,
till even the chase overtakes me
and moves farther away
as the husk moves from the fruit seed,
until the running
catches up within itself, and stops.
And I will collapse there
like a young man meeting his love.

V.

And after I have let the running
overtake me, after
still moving in itself, it stops
like a stone,
or like quicksilver
behind the glass of a mirror,
I will watch myself in all things,
I will embrace within me
all things at once,
and they
will cast me back, long after
all that was some *thing* in me
has passed into other things.

VI.

Here I am
remaining what I am,
running back towards myself
with flags of solitude, with shields of cold,
tearing myself away from everywhere,
tearing myself away from in front of me,
from behind me, from my right,
from my left, from above me
and from beneath me, going out
from everywhere and everywhere leaving
things to be remembered:
stars to the sky,
air to the earth,
branches with leaves to the shadows.

VII.

. . . strange body, asymmetrical body
astonished at itself
in the presence of spheres,

astonished when facing the sun,
patiently waiting for the light
to grow the appropriate body.

VIII.

To lean on your own earth
when you are seed, when winter
liquifies its long white bones
and spring rises.

To lean on your own land
when you are alone, when you are spent

by lack of love,
or simply when winter
decomposes, and spring
moves its spherical space
like a heart
toward its rhythmic corners.

Purified to enter
the labors of spring,
to tell the seeds that they are seeds,
to tell the earth that it is earth!

But before everything
we are seeds, we are those
seen from all sides at once,
as though we lived deep in an eye,
or a field, where instead of grass
glances are growing — and now we,
hardened, almost metallic,
we harvest the blades of grass, so that they
will be like all other things
in whose center we live,
and which were born from our heart.

But before everything
we are seeds, and we prepare ourselves
to throw ourselves out of ourselves into something else,
something much higher, something
called spring . . .
To be inside the phenomena,
always inside them.

To be seed and to lean
on your own earth.

THREE

a selection from

Epica Magna
1978

her

Only now, only now
when I love her the most,
only now I lie to her.
Only now, only now
when she thinks of me the most,
I don't care.
Only now, only now
when she thinks of me
I whistle in vain.
Only now, only now
when she is the most beautiful
among my stars,
am I blind.
Only now, only now
when I feel her gracefulness
piercing the walls of the city
am I deaf.
Only now, only now
when I know she misses me
I insult my friends
because I cannot bear wanting her.
Only now, only now
when she irons
her plaid dress for me,
I use gasoline to clean spears
to throw at animals and vultures.
Only now, only now
when I should run away,
I prolong my sleep
afraid to be happy.
Only now, only now
when light comes from her breast,

I read about stars exploding
and I sprawl
like the longest street in town
and I pave and dress myself
in snow and ice,
mostly ice,
because I want her to slip
while crossing the street
and hurt her ankle,
which, God,
I haven't kissed for so long.
Because after all,
who has the guts to kiss an ankle
that doesn't limp?!

confession

I still cannot raise a hymn
to the silence I need, and for which I am hungry.
No house where I lived
has kept me long.
I wish I could live
inside my words,
but my body feels heavy
and hangs through doors, towards the kingdom of animals.
I would be happy to give dogs what is theirs
and to horses what belongs to them,
but the barking of dogs is unheard,
and the smell of horses forbidden.
I must move much higher,
but I am disturbed by the thought,—
that what is up there
is the same as down here,—
and I learn
that each cast has no direction,
and that each denial is static.

why?

If one must clean the water,—
what kind of water
should one use
to clean it?
Oh, you made me believe the word,—
that is how I was born and I will die:
Oh, you made me believe that I am the word,
and the word, is you.

Why did you make the grass,
I am asking you—
and why did you make the horse,
the mosquitoes, the polecats,
why did you make them?
Why did you make the tree,
to humiliate me, why?
. . . to spit on me, you made
the mouse, the pig, the dog,
and I am asking why?

Oh, I believed that I exist
for the word that you were supposed to drink
without being thirsty! . . .

Why did you make the rock stale,
and why did you make me
and give me wings to fly above it,
why?

contemplating the world from the outside

Part I: THE TERRESTRIAL NERVE

1. *The one who died about the still unborn*

We need a time to reconcile
our way of being,
a time to give light to our eyes,
eyes which began to grow the wrong way
upon our entire beings,
eyes growing from nostrils and fingers,
thick eyes growing from heels,
the same eyes
which under the strange aspect of words
and screams
we get rid of.

He will be sight
we know this,
he will be sight.
This is why we already prepared
the beds of our eyes
in which there are no tears.
For him we keep them clean, without tears,
whenever he needs to pass the night,
whenever he might come
whenever he will arrive.

2. *The terrestrial nerve*

This is the first part of the description:
here, in this cosmic zone

under the blue eyelid,
they all eat each other.
Man eats the bird,
the bird eats the worm,
the worm eats the grass,
the grass eats the remains of man,
the remains of man eat the stone,
the stone eats the water,
the fire eats the air,
the air eats the earth.

This is the way, plenty of food,
which never ends.

The characteristic noise
is that of jaws, their chewing.

This is the idea:
the largest dimension in space
                        is the point.
One is not larger than the other.
The mountain is a point
and the blade of grass is also a point.

This is the belief:
for a long time the food
which feeds itself
which is nourishment for the food,
which is satisfied with food
would have ended in this blue point.
Yet light comes from outside,
yet blind radiation comes from outside.

At the bottom of this hunger,
at the bottom of this endless hunger
is the light from outside,
the blind radiation from outside
which, when added to the one eaten,

replaces
the eaten part.

3. *The terrestrial phonetics*

Each covering is different:
grass for earth,
water for fish,
fur and skin for flesh,
the shout for fright,
letters for the word,
and, at the end, everywhere, the air.

4. *The terrestrial morphology*

Water forms the majority.
Because of this,
during the general starvation,
it occupies a distinguished place
called the general thirst.

In return, it drinks and eats everything.
Seen from the distance,
there is no distinction
between people, animals and plants.
It is a planet, big as a point
on which different points
think themselves to be owners.
From the distance,
one cannot judge
who owns the planet,
which point owns the point.

However, one can conclude, that they all have something
in common
which is the belly, the stomach.

Around the stomach
some grew leaves,
some grew wings,
some grew a brain.
Yet, from the distance,
there is almost no distinction
between what grew
around one stomach
or what grew around another.

Every belly has the same hunger
proven by the fact that they eat each other,
the proof that they exist.

5. *The terrestrial syntax*

Although all beings and things
on earth
live in a permanent blending

although everything is just an endless meal,
although from space, from far away
all of them, together, appear to have a single life,
although from far away, from very far away
space is only filled
by a delicate whisper
of jaws and gums,
that of roots and waves
chewing

although even this cannot have
a particular aspect,
one can say
without being mistaken
that a certain order
and a certain settlement exists there

Because, always someone
                    eats
somebody else is eaten.

Part II: THE DIVINE NERVE

1. *The still unborn about the dead*

This blue colored point
which calls itself earth
is the eye
is the formal bed
is the bed of leisure
belonging generally to sight.

From a distance,
from a very great distance,
the birth of the world and its future
are glued
and sleep is embraced in this
                    blue point.

Here all the meals
embrace each other
and all the faces
are superimposed

Here all the numbers sleep
in the number one,
and the number one sleeps
in this blue point

Here the infinite seen from the infinite
is a point

This is the only tragic place

because the number one rules,
and not zero,
because loneliness rules,
and not nothing,
because death rules,
and not the spirit.
Despair rules here,
and not emptiness.

This is the point,
this is the divine blue point
heart of all hearts
body of all bodies
and the drained blood
from all cosmic wounds.

This is the cemetery
where the bone of the star Antares
has been buried.
This is the crib
where the fatherless child
of the star Arcturus
screams and wrestles.

2. *The divine nerve*

This is the second part of the description:
under the blue eyelid
here in this cosmic zone
all are born from all.
Man is born from the bird,
the bird from the worm,
the worm from the grass,
grass from the remains of man,
the birth of man from dead grass,
the death of the stone from grass born,
the birth of the stone from dead water.

All in one
placing their bodies from one end to the other
knotted with deathly rings.
This is the idea:
the largest domain
is life
no life is larger than another,
no death remains unadorned
by a birth.

This is the belief:
time is created here without stop,
time is produced,
one kills and gives birth to time
one eats time,
one sells time,
one deposits time,
one wastes time,
one saves time.

From far away
from very far away
this blue point
could be confused
with time.

3. *The song*

It interrupts
any other move.

It makes that which exists
vanish
makes appear in being
what is still unborn.

It turns everything into sight
and makes the light hungry.

It swings death
until words bloom
and adorn the laws of fixed stars
with tears.
This at times is called the soul,
but it would be even more precise to call it
song.

4. *The singer*

Nobody needs him
yet there is no way without him.

Tell us how we eat each other,
he is told:—and make us cry!

He knows everyone's cry
and the tear they ought to have.

Among people, on earth,
singers are born.
Among grass, too.
And among animals,
stone,
fish,
water,
air,
fire,
singers are born.

Everything on earth
at one time or another needs to cry.

5. *The significance*

Here is the end
of our computer report.
All the cards
with their necessary information
have been processed.
Seen from the outside,
the characteristic of the people
and that of the inhabitants
found on the blue point
is that they exist
and can create a strange feeling,
that tendency *to be*.

The spatial lost within them
is the light from other, different stars.

They produce, in exchange, time
for space.

the sky's mistake

The vultures were flying upside down
and with upturned claws
want to steal the star and its wavy light
the way they steal sheep;

The light from my eyes
is like sheep stolen from above.

All over the sky
vultures were flying upside down
and their spines fell
touching my chest.

My flesh was their sky,
the light from my eyes
their earth.

hieroglyphics

How lonely
not to understand
when there is meaning

And how lonely
to be blind in the middle of the day,—
and to be deaf, in the middle of song
how lonely

But not to understand
when there is no meaning
and to be blind at midnight
and deaf when the silence is perfect,—
Oh, most lonely of the lonely!

FOUR

a selection from

Operele Imperfecte

Imperfect Works
1979

lesson on the cube

You take a piece of stone,
you carve it with a chisel made of blood,
you polish it with Homer's eye,
and shine it even more with light,
until the cube is perfect.
Then you kiss the cube several times
with your mouth and the mouths of others
and especially with the mouth of an infant.
Then suddenly you take a hammer
and smash a corner of the cube.
Everybody, everybody will say:
— What a perfect cube this would have been
without a broken corner!

talking

Do you think the grass is happy?
It is green; it is green . . .
Do you think the eagle is high?
He is flying; he is flying . . .
Do you think the stone is silent?
It is hard; it is hard . . .
Do you think that I am yours?
Do you think so?

untitled

The king never
has the right to dance before the throne.
Never will sadness
wear its own crown.
The eye never
has the right to be blind.
Never will my mother
give birth again.
The stone never
will be soft nor will it flow.
Never, never,
never.

the keys

From the stars a chain of keys fell through my brain,
my mind was a jingle of pain and sound.
My entire body became a key of iron,
god, for a gigantic door
whose lock I cannot reach,
unless you lift me in your arms.
Come, as great as you are,
come, as indifferent as you are,
twist me and break me
and open that door at once!
Come, and open that door at once!

transfiguration of the face

I exchanged birth for death,
For the rest I remained poor.
An angel struck me with his wing
and I became a king,
on a throne collapsing.
I do not know what five is,
I do not know what four is
in fact, I do not know anything,
but I confess that my crown is tight,
friends, my temples are like an horizon,
my crown like a star or a bullet,
straight in the forehead.

engagement

He didn't dare come home.
His wife, made more beautiful from loneliness,
had become his bride.
She held on her left ear
a two-winged butterfly
and was trying but not able to cry;—
its spirit had a scent like lavender,
and the air was like all birds flying!
She was lying down and white—
on her finger the fallen wedding ring
shined like a comet.

the ghost

What a strange church
with bells stuck in the ground!
Church that had descending stairs
not having *to be*.
Beggars with bending heads
were praying to a potato,
to a worm.
You, church harnessed
to the earth's angels,
ploughing my words . . .
And all the bells, showing
their tongues to the stars,
as if talking.
The ghost with feet on the sky
is running.

the lark

They began to polish my coffin
And will bury me in a cloud
which will rain with the dead.
Touch the back of my neck mother
even if it gets wet with blood.
Believe me mother, the dead man can rain
but does not cry.
The angel struck my back mother,
not in a pleasing way
but in a silent one.
I forgot myself mother
that's why I die, that's why I have died.

lesson on the circle

On the sand you draw a circle
which you divide in two,
with the same stick of almond you divide that in two.
Then you fall on your knees,
and then you fall on your arms.
And after that you strike your forehead on the sand
and ask the circle to forgive you.
So much.

Nichita Stănescu, Romania's leading contemporary poet, was born in Ploiești in 1933. He attended the University of Bucharest and graduated with a degree in philosophy in 1957. Currently, he lives in Bucharest where he works as an editor for *România literară*. His second book, *O Viziune a Sentimentelor,* (A Sentimental Vision) won the first prize from the Writers' Union. Since that time, Mr. Stănescu has been the recipient of many honors for his poetry. In 1971, he was invited to read his poems at the Poetry International festival in London; in 1976 he was awarded the *Herder Prize* in Vienna; and in 1982, the *Gold Wreath for Poetry* from Yugoslavia. Most recently, his work has appeared in leading journals throughout the United States and England. His poetry has been translated into several languages.